Dance

First published in 2011
by Wayland



Wayland
338 Euston Road
London NW1 3BH

Wayland Australia
Level 17/207 Kent Street
Sydney, NSW 2000



Series Editor: Louise John
Editor: Katie Woolley
Design: D.R.ink
Consultant: Shirley Bickler
Photographer: Andy Crawford

A CIP catalogue record for this book is available
from the British Library.

ISBN 9780750264983

Printed in China

Wayland is a division of Hachette Children's Books,
an Hachette UK Company

www.hachette.co.uk

The Publisher and author would like to thank the staff and pupils at Dance In Fusion The Academy.

# Contents

# My dance class

My name is Adrianna
and today I am going
to my dance class.

# Getting ready

I put on my t-shirt and jazz pants. I pack my jazz shoes and make sure my hair is neat and tidy.

## Top Tips

**It is important to have neat and tidy hair when you are dancing so that it doesn't get in your eyes.**

I take a drink and my tracksuit
for after the class.

# The teacher

Mum is taking me to dance class today.

My dance class is at our village hall.
Lisa is my teacher. She is teaching
us street dance.

# Meeting my friends

I go to dance class once a week after school. Mum drops me off.

I say hello to my friends. There are six of us in our class.

# The warm-up

We start with a warm-up.
Lisa puts on some music
and we stand in lines.

Then we start to march
and jog on the spot.

**Top Tips**

**It is important to warm up before dancing.**

# Stretches

We skip or jog round the room
and do star jumps.

Then we do some stretches. Stretching before dance is important as it helps to stop us getting hurt.

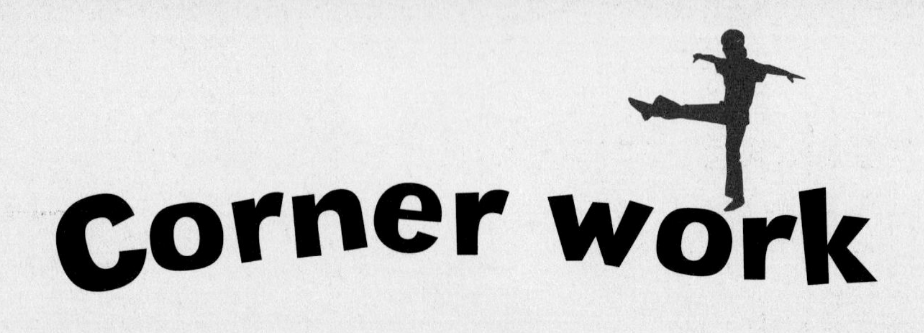

# Corner work

Next we do corner work. First we practise our step kicks.

We have to hold our arms out and try and keep our legs straight as we kick.

# Step turns

Next we do some step turns.

## Top Tips

**Keeping your eyes on one spot as you turn will stop you getting dizzy.**

Lisa tells me to remember to keep my eyes on one spot.

# The show

Then it is time to rehearse for the show that we are putting on at Christmas.

We learn just one part. Lisa shows us the steps and then we practise them.

# Taking a break

Sometimes we stop to have a break and drink some water.

**Top Tips**

**Always drink plenty of water when you get hot.**

Then Lisa shows us the costumes we will be wearing for the show.

# The dance

After our break, we get into two groups. We have to dance in front of the others.

My group has to dance first while
the other group watches us.

# Practice

Then we change over and
we watch the other group.

It helps us because we
can spot things that
make our dancing better.

# The best dancer

At the end of the lesson, Lisa tells us
we are doing very well.

Every week the group picks the best dancer. I am really happy because this week they pick me!

# Time to go home

It is time to go home. I tell my friends I will see them next week.

Mum is here to pick me up.
I can't wait for my dance
class next week!

**START READING** is a series of highly enjoyable books for beginner readers. **The books have been carefully graded to match the Book Bands widely used in schools.** This enables readers to be sure they choose books that match their own reading ability.

**Look out for the Band colour on the book in our Start Reading logo.**

The Bands are:

**START READING** books can be read independently or shared with an adult. They promote the enjoyment of reading through satisfying stories, plays and non-fiction narratives, which are supported by fun illustrations and photographs.

**Jillian Powell** has written many fiction and non-fiction books for children. She began writing stories when she was just four years old and she hasn't stopped since! She lives in a house beside a village church and still sits down to write every day.